Poppy's Leavetaking

POPPY'S LEAVETAKING
New Poems

Tom Mac Intyre

NEW ISLAND

POPPY'S LEAVETAKING
First published 2012
by New Island
2 Brookside
Dundrum Road
Dublin 14

www.newisland.ie

Copyright © Tom Mac Intyre, 2012

The author has asserted his moral rights.

PRINT ISBN: 978-1-84840-204-1

All rights reserved. The material in this publication is protected by copyright law. Except as may be permitted by law, no part of the material may be reproduced (including by storage in a retrieval system) or transmitted in any form or by any means; adapted; rented or lent without the written permission of the copyright owner.

British Library Cataloguing Data. A CIP catalogue record for this book is available from the British Library.

Typeset by Mariel Deegan
Cover design by Sinéad McKenna
Printed by SPRINT-print Ltd

New Island received financial assistance from
The Arts Council (An Chomhairle Ealaíon), Dublin, Ireland.

10 9 8 7 6 5 4 3 2 1

For Céline

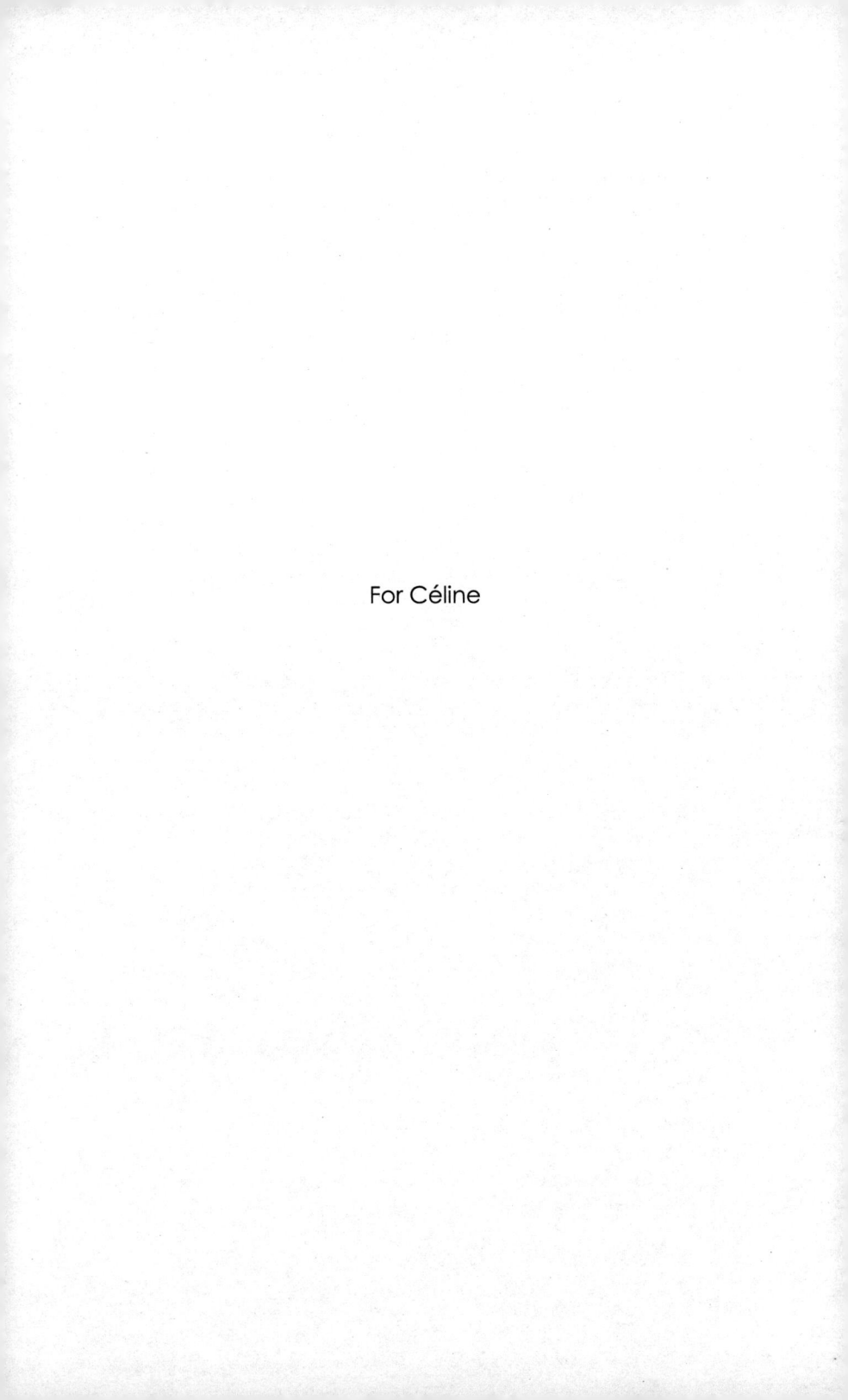

Acknowledgements are due here to the editors of the following publications in which some of these poems first appeared:

Cyphers, Irish Pages, Poetry Ireland, and *The Irish Times.*

Contents

1. Meeting The Stone	1
2. Sister	3
3. The Mountains	4
4. The Boat	5
5. Points of View	6
6. Message to Bernini	7
7. Puppet	8
8. The Canton of *La Marge*	10
9. Mountain Dew	11
10. Feathers, Chosen	12
11. Things Come By Threes (Or Fours)	14
12. Dark Angel's Word, And	16
13. What The Cat-Scan Said	17
14. My Angelica	18
15. Snapshot	20
16. Aisling Eile	22
17. Conversazione	24
18. The Far East	25
19. Pangur Buí	26
20. Blackberries, Vicarstown	29
21. The Burning	31
22. Stiff-Neck	32
23. Spade & Sea	34
24. The Wasp	35
25. Rubato	37
26. Embrace	41
27. Initiant	43
28. Poppy's Leavetaking	44
29. Found In A Suitcase	46
30. Observations	47
31. At The Butt of the Lane	49

32. The Honey   50
33. Brosna means 'kindling'   51
34. Immersion   52
35. Those Ants   53
36. The Possible   54
37. La Vie Bohème   55
38. Uncle Tim   57
39. Such A Time With The Swan   58
40. Her Bright Scissors   60
41. The Storm   61
42. The Portrait Hour   62

1 | Meeting The Stone

Stone nourishes now an imp:
for cap today blunt kitchen knife,
handle toward my hand (old
Stratford trick), he's more than lump.

Takes an ojus span taming a stone,
cloud your window'd heart to hear him moan.

Years back cliff-top boulder –
'Watch it, Micko, I'm *capo di capi*.'
Fallow for periods, always there.

While I seek to cope with his
morning coup, comes a screech
of rain, lands me on a saddle-
ridge of Brandon, lost and found,
October, say, seventeen twenty-four.
A notice points – *The Height The Soldier Fell*.
I can see miles and miles of the main.

Takes an ojus span tamin' a stone,
work you he will to the parent bone.

A prayer, loose,
loose a prayer,
find the words,
make them fit,
words for chisel,
muscle and chisel
knit, hammer sweet,
an' breathin' from
the diaphragm,

ar nós, ar nós,
ar nós whom,
do you suppose?

Eibhlín Dhubh, say, or Eoghan Rua,
or, bless him, that rogue Cathal Buí...

2 | Sister

Nor secateur kiss, nor time of day,
colour of night, rose descended
like a puzzle solved, petals
weightless, sonsy, every

last one first: caught,
as never before, smell
of my clay, fragrance of yours, child-

woman allowed narrow room here,
could have loved you more,

couldn't I, and you
restored now, petals,
petals under the tree.

3 | The Mountains

Easy to forget where you live.
Venture abroad this day –
'And you're from?' 'The mountains.'
How they stare. Everywhere

you look mountains, Cavan
mountains, Monaghan,
Fermanagh, Leitrim, Down
mountains, Gullion, The Cooleys,
pre-birth the mountains own us.

We set out, climb, trek
the last pig-back ridge,
gauge shifts of the corrie lake.
And the fish jumps, bidden.

Coming down is the hard bit,
the mountains want you to stay.
Useful note: *early is late*.
No time, tossed, find your-
self back where you started

4 | The Boat

Boat leaves the quay,
quay dwindles like never was,
he's there to starboard,
fine cut of a lad,
hurley in hand,

throws up the sliotar,
belts it landward,

watch him now,
he's only startin' –

the hurley's after it,
hurley too in flight,

there's a sea-bird
not yet known,
there's a sight,

curve of the ash,
battle-seasoned,

ascending,
descending,

and, how like a prayer,
she kisses the tide.

5 | Points of View

'For the eyes there's a desert age brings,'
he speaks: cooped in the chair, I listen,
'Sight's fine, just that needful springs go
dry. Lack of irrigation

will cause discomfort, or worse, pain,
chronic, could be.' 'There's no cure?'
'Try your luck. Drops, faux moisture,
for sale by the hundred. Legerdemain

to a chemist smile. We're dodgy clay.'
Rain on the window. As Wrinkly dumps guise
of the forsaken – 'What price tears of joy,
balm unrivalled for desert-weary eyes?'

Our quiet spins. *Come on, give it a go.*
'Why not' – at last – 'if you've found it so.'

6 | Message to Bernini

Ghian Lorenzo Bernini,
you said it all,

my beloved's
beauty flows from those lips
almost parted –

as tho' she were
about to speak:

from those same lips
almost closed –

she's just spoken,
weft of her words

intemperate woodbine
'round and about me,
body and soul.

7 | Puppet

He depends
on the strings,
God knows it shows

on his skin,
in the bockety limbs,
medieval grimace,
Sweet Christ, it shows,

no let-up,
no, nay, never,
tada, tada, tada,

something else
while we're at it,
he has this song –
the *singing puppet!* –

but, for all his
bravery, make that plural,
it – it – it lacks
the least sign
of – all right, it's a whine.

It's The Wail,
from Doneraile.

Ould Son,
beware the storm,

tyrant hands
going for it again,

(must you sing?
I'll pay you
not to sing),

Caveat Emptor,
old adviser,
is there a door
against the storm?

Up/down
in/out
left/right
shit/shite
day/night

please don't sing
please don't gulder

8 | The Canton of *La Marge*

Cow-Parsley took me by the throat.
'Am I,' she enquires, 'was I –
when? – the summer-scented innocent
of popular imagination, how
could you – thrapple calcify? –
howsomever swallow such smarm?'
In all this I knew she was right.
'*Colour supplement* your middle name?'

'Have you forgotten my lick of sulphur?
Why, Sir, the tag *Devil's Oatmeal*?
Adder's Meat? May I emblazon
a few honourable slurs? I been
called *Hemlock*, *Dog's Keck* – sure,
as in *Dog's Keck*, *Scabby Hands*,
no less, on a regular basis,
and witches, I'll have you know, Sir,
hail hog's dung – and me!'
in all that I knew that she was right.

'Sorry to seem bit of a barge.
You don't seem to have heard of,'
wickedly she pursued, 'are you hard
of hearing, perhaps, no one ever
speak to you, cadenced voice, of
the fusty ample canton of *La Marge*?
Home of the rare ingot your canton of *La Marge*.'

'Where do I find the canton of *La Marge*?'
I caught in my voice a ragged beat.
Cow-Parsley, leaving, said, 'Child At Large,
look for it under the soles of your feet.'

9 | Mountain Dew

On the slopes early,
late March morning,
I'm brought to a whirly
halt, it was surprising

and not, cameo of this
strappin' young hare erect
on sweet designer pegs,
topaz lift to the coat,

poised above the furze
bush, that vanguard yellow;
through a birthing haze
of ponder and stop-go

signage, behold me
beauty leaning to sip –
oh, so, so *raffiné* –
from cup, cup after cup

of the copious blossom.
I stand imperfectly still;
somewhere nigh, a home.
You can hear the well.
Transyescendental.

Did it alter my life?
Sure. Did for a while.

10 | Feathers, Chosen

Fairy-tale bed of the Granny
lesson'd you first magic of *feather*,
power of air, freedom from gravity,
but our sin's to disremember;

now, hundred years or more
later, I'm in loopy flight next
the dove, *mein liebling*, matter
of substance finds a way – *shapeshift* –
fingerclick – how'd I gather

a scissors, such cavalier daring,
to trim a handful of feathers
from breast of the soul-bird, living
it up, the pair of us, makin' space,
it's there, wide as all outdoors,

my dove, *cool*, man, continues
on course, they do, will, must,
continuant is their airy compass,
contiguous the pulse of those
wings, wasn't dove born, first
day, I've heard it said, contaygious
to The Templed Nile? She's *gift*.

*****

For sequel? They're with me this
minute, breast-feathers of the bird,
companionable to my left,
we collogue, morbidezza, need

I say. Ever lose them, shed
interest, find other passthetimes?
Like it that you ask the toughest
question, road to l'arnin'. I did, yes,
bottle it, find other recreations.

And? That was *nel mezzo, nel
mezzo*, it's agreed, takes forever,
fearsome pong belly of the whale,
hair bombed white, innards fungal,
and, one day, the wraparound whack:
'Room only for one on the ladder.
Plus, Micko, no turning back.'

One Canossa of a scourge, good ould
rehab. Takes. Takes. Takes more.
Nuzzle the wood's obsidian core.
Now in love with those feathers
again, I hear good Granny Gillick's
slubbed snore. Hear Imminence.
Immanence. So much happens
contaygious to The Templed Nile.

Were I not forbidden (baldly) converse
with my beautiful grand-daughters,
I would sing them power of air,
freedom from gravity, sins of disremember.

11 | Things Come By Threes (Or Fours)

They named the Care-Home *Avalon*
(winner, short-head, from *Elysium*).
Gimcrack chic absorbs the waiting-room.
Thru the window, foot-path zone,
 two young lassies skipping, been
there forever, figuring eights, circles,
ovals, skipping, skipping, heedless
 of all but their lives, pending...

Now you arrive, ever *The Only Girl*,
your load of years a delicate
vase, untried hands furtive, fretful,
nails a mess, and bling bling still
bling – I salute such *No Surrender*.
Betty's with you, thirty years your
junior, sturdy Betty has lost it,
wears qui vive of the lost, listens:
miles and miles away, unruly school
playground, her children shouting, hear
them sometimes, often, a far singing...

An hour ago, March full moon
breadth of the window as I write,
one of those dreams that must,
the while I breathe, never wane:
two young women, laughing flowers,
the two communing, mixum of that
and self-communing, they're abrimmin',

say nothing, there's naught to say,
scarcely move, but their pavane

goes on and on, beyond haste,
they know, conceive no other play,
won't seek such. Now they melt.
And seems I'll never dream again.

You recall an hour, ripe of the moon
leaning to homage lovely bared breast,
sleeping breasts, of The Woman lost. And won.

12 | Dark Angel's Word, And

'Come thou art flesh, thou hast
overcome thy mighty entertainment' –

The Maestro of Seething Ambages,
that's all right, that's fine,
knife – change not a phrase –
knife it on the immaterial stone,

but with this proviso:
leave room for the face,
thieved from some Etruscan
hoard, of The One, She who,
giving, bared her breast
once, mid-stairway, offered
the mole, sanctioned the kiss,
and The Dunce, adrift,
content with a glance,
humped off to dine,
at an empty board.

She who, no more than an hour
since, texts – 'The dark tendril's tresses
that were so bright' – that's her! –
glossolalia me that, yer Trinity Scholars,

must wait, can't wait, to kiss
that mole, yield it my fresher lips,
honestly, to a sigh, unhurried –
that sigh the word for *Yes* –
then to Her meadow, with it said.

13 | What The Cat-Scan Found

Two leaves loose in my hair,
one red, one green, the duo
scalloped, oily, every way taking.

That wunderkind again, super-
market trolley for cradle –
wunderbar, wunderbar, wunderbar –
'Patience,' says she, 'is ever gain.'
And the behemoth barks –
'Breathe in. Breathe out. *Slán*.'

Down a shadowy lane
of the car-park, stained
catacomb usually devoid
of catechumen or numen,

a white horse,
bridled, saddled,
shy, notably shy.

14 | My Angelica

Dusk. The garden.
Behold. Your beloved
Angelica is wrecked,
how'd that happen?

Action: container
melts, moulded clay
glows, juicy sculpture
in bald display.

Action: nether regions,
from clay's nether
zone, horns protrude:
give you one guess:
horns of the impenitent
tenant-at-will Lord
Grub, horns off-white
or baby-blue, could
be, mutant snouts
testing the view.

Bow, bow, Sir,
to your Control-Tower,
your Ash-Cloud,
your Stella's Bower
and Petrified Wood,

how they sway,
grotesque, ordinary,
laxadaisy,

and now enter –
not a moment –
not one – too soon,
stage right, left,
and still centre,
the sickle moon.

15 | Snapshot

You'd take a keen
hard look at this
specimen fram'd in kitchen
doorway, caught, he's else-
where, also, that's the bother,

he's somewhere else
entirely, with his
body-guard pallor,
fret (*na mná*, likely,
na mná), unholy
fret and cheek-bone
sheen from the far
side of a steep ravine,

you'd mutter a prayer
if you've one to spare
this passing and blessed
minute, go a tad better,
have Masses read,

were it not, were it
not, unsurely, for that
armful of turf held
warm to the breast,

were it not for
the rings, those rings,
one dark, one bright,
on the choiring ring-

fingers, the bracelet,
amber, on the left
wrist, with lantern shine.

16 | Aisling Eile

My meadow strolls. I give you
a drop-dead beautiful woman,
sorrel, sorrel abundant, unruly,
sprouting/swaying from her sonsy
anus, and world, worlds, begin anew.

It was not the moment for tact,
we made, at once, boldly, our
desires plain, and, hail sweet thunder,
she gives consent. Presto, it's *hot*.

Sweat on the pliant hanches, sweat
the hinges, wordless, breathless,
suckin' diesel. Comes the exotic bit,
our twist on poor ould tristesse.

There we are, natt'rin' about the weather,
grand little country but for et
cetera, when I twig, will forever,
a sorrel leaf, Jesus, losing it,

its green's a jewel, its lightness
morphing to a breath, a vapour,
glimmer, bamboozalem – guess –
what next, I'm front-row viewer

of sorrel leaf in melt-down mode,
watching – close-up – first leaf ever
tear off the veils – becoming a jazz
riff, Blake on speed, Leonardo –

'Let's go,' I hear the maiden's voice.
And we go. Off we go.

17 | Conversazione

What I love about meetings
with long-departed kith or kin
is how spare the utterance,

everything's thin as a latch,
everything trimm'd to the bone –
'Hey, did you watch the match?'

And it's true, they *are* wiser,
aren't they? The very last question
I'd have forecast but, whether
or which, only question, sheer
question, *all* questions – win,
lose, abstain. 'Did you bother,
Wrinkly, to watch? Cup the pain?'

Habits we fashion here so rough,
rug-headed. I loved her rune,
opal, where it boldly led,
loved her to death, answered
freely – 'Yes. It was tough.'

18 | The Far East

There was a magazine
in the long ago wuz called
The Far East –

an' what was that magazine
attempin' for te propergate?

The Converzhin, if ye doan' mind,
o' them haythen hordes
along the banks o' the Yangadzee River.

Yed see it in school,
come wance a month,
open it up, there they are,
lukin out at ye, the faces

o' them haythen hordes,
waitin' for te be baptised
along the banks o' the Yangadzee River –

Glory be to Christ,
The Far East –

19 | Pangur Buí

Hail dreaming spires of Lurganboy,
and townlands adjacent likewise:
he's my University, I major in joy.

It's the surrender – when he hunts,
the cosmos is chase; when he eats,
first meal ever laid on platter,
and when he sleeps, ah, lend your
roomy eyes as Suitor Morpheus
presents him chaise-longue so rare –
foam-sprung, air-borne, Welcome, Lover –

you fear it's sleep for aye –
but know it isn't, it's for Pangur
Buí – alone – this exemplary
embrace. And, mark you, never a snore.

Time's are when (scissors/Vet)
I grieve his diminished plight,
such curt demise of caterwaul:
Pussy in rut, rinsing the night,
Pangur antiphonal, I'm en route,
this gism, Honey, super chrism –

Then I think, we accommodate,
don't we, Surgery snip doesn't
seem to bother Pangur one whit,

mere bagatelle,
a conjurer's trick;
Explorer, *circumspice*,
everywhere marvel!

Don't know how you do it,
Pangur, tell me, explain –
you are telling me – I don't
attend – there's my chronic sin –

But Pangur, listen,
isn't memory
one hellova
Golgotha? Do *you* remember,
do you? Scrub the question,
I know you do, total recall,
I'll shut up now for a while,

cool this hour
and thole the next
as dry longevity –
our new elixir –
permits me to oversee
a withered tree.

'Rejoice, rejoice,'
Pangur's in like a flash,
'You've still leave to piss!'

Those Cambodian wizard eyes
engage indolent surprise,
urge you, Red-Neck, to be wise.

Stasis. Stasis. Stasis.
'Still leave to piss.'

I extend a contrite hand –
may I? – we hover – shape –
permission granted – I bend
to caress, in high humility,
that quattrocento nape ...

Pangur, Pangur, Sage of Lurganboy,
you're my University, I major in joy.

20 | Blackberries, Vicarstown

A van large outside the door.
Navy blue rectangular block
of it says, first gear – 'There y'are.'

Knew at a glance it was full
to the brim of Demeter's black pearls,
fruit, yes, of my harvesting,
knew also at a glance the cargo
was bound for The Faraway. Court-
esy call? Looked like. Say hello –

'What route are you taking?' I ask
the driver, first question came into
my gob. Whole thing happen again,
might ask some other. Or say nothin'.
'We go,' said he, 'through Vicarstown.'

The answer came casual, loaded,
jewelled, plain, Marriage Announcement,
Obitnoticey, Birth of First Child Three
Days Ago. 'All roads lead' I chanced,
'to Vicarstown?' He began his beguine.
A wave. Then the gate. Gone.

And I'm left, contented harvester.
I thought – payback, thought August,
stooped trance of the ditches, thought
bring them, bring them home to Her,
black pearls of August, lottery
offerings of October. And, again, trance.

A woman curious, young and fair,
asked me once – 'Tranced sex. What's
that?' 'Tranced' I told her, 'trance
is daze, happenstance – and prayer.'

21 | The Burning

My altar's patient in the field,
tidy rock, scattershot where
we live. The shirt, well-informed,
must go. Good innings. Au revoir.

Its demise (you find this with
letters also, diaries?), demise
a hapless screech, quick death,
no, revise: God's truth is
it varies; silk, poplin, synthetic
this or that, weather conditions
will also intrude, finally lick
an' a prayer; known, even, a kiss –
call it Imagination, if you please –
whirr from the smoke, chequered flame –
loth, is it? – someone, Eros to erase?

Burned many a shirt, boat,
one or two houses, in my prime.
At droll intervals, sure, penitent.
Sackcloth? Fasting? Perhaps – but lite.
Maybe, people say, you were born lame?
Simple – could be – simple as that.

More and more I focus the one kiss,
our heroine of the fire, loth,
aye, diamond-loth, Eros to erase.
Caught once, of late, her sweet breath.

Is, ar Éireann, ní'neosfainn cé hí.

22 | Stiff-Neck

'For some enduring good,
ask, ask, your Tiger,
consult your Butterfly,'
mantra of the doctor
who arrives regularly
to lance the neck, let blood,

the lance, flux, is
prologue, the cure *poetry*,
neck thaws as we compose,
as weeks, months, go by
under skies of pouty
marl, spare Viking blues,

as Matt The Post questions
what I'm thinking about
while he loiters by the rowan,
lantern-jaws berry-bright,
he knows 'I do be at
the writin',' words, words,
hears that faraway ukase –

'Thinkin', Mattie and no lie,
*Ask, ask The Tiger, consult
Invalid, your Butterfly.*'

Mattie takes a long look
at Sliabh na Cailligh's
undulant noblesse:
the cairns loose a cardiac
humming, limitless...

'See ye the morra, Boss.
An' shur keep winnin'.'

The green van shrugs,
scatters grit, flows into
the next honeyed lane.

23 | Spade & Sea

The spade hurls at you, blade
zapping the water, leaving for track
a nuptial of sparks, harvest & seed;

knew at once spade had your number,
ditto the lickety-spit galloon of sparks,
equally well-informed our salt-water;

for a wink seem'd they'd traffick
thru you for a short-cut but
no – swerve balletic, a-jink, a-jook,

Spade and Gobán train skirl
past, and out of sight,
the *Express*, not the *Local*.

You consigned yourself to Twitter glow.
This very morning knew. Saw. Know.

The spade. Salt-water. Galloon of sparks.
This morning opened for you. The works.

Enabled fair consent. April consent.

24 | The Wasp

We have previous. Previous
of a serious nature. Eleven,
twelve, on a scale of ten.

I killed her – only
you can't ever kill
wasp, her lives too many
for your crass disposal.

Even as I lost it –
dirty bed, sour season –
I knew she was right,
she'd mapped my unreason.

All, all returned
last night – I find her,
took twenty years, more,
playing my left hand,
knew, in deeps, I'm forgiven,
seem'd I never wore
black and yellow before,
music in colour, Chopin.

'In the female, a stinging
organ, for purpose fit' –
maybe I've learned to shiver?
'That be true,' I inquire,
'long latter end learned to shiver?'
I wait. Music. Chopin –

Chopin, it's said, who
arrived in Paris
with only two possessions –
'*Le froid. Et l'inconnu.*'

25 | Rubato

That stone. Stone
dead ringer for
a rabbit? Or, or
rabbit dead ringer
for lithe stone?

Or rabbit asleep?
It's bedamnable close,
fug of heat-haze.
Or *glic* rabbit
in pretend doze?
They would teach
you your prayers.

I hold still,
not a gig. The stone
(if stone it be)
doesn't stir, like-
wise the rabbit
(if such it truly
be). All quiet.

Is this then
what they mean by
'suspended animation',

a weather I've
never before known,
not at this pitch,
certainly, has me on
a high I'll remember

a long day, I know
that, meanwhile
your next move?
Your move, Sir?

But is it? My
move. Yes, it is.
Rabbit won't, stone
can't. Yes, it is,

your call, Micko,
in this grassy
plot among the whins,
the dozing whins...

It's a rabbit for
sure, a rabbit's
forty winks. Or – or
Bugs Mac Glic
in faux torpor...

Yet – and yet –
fair possibility –
your lithe stone,
taking it easy?
Taking it slow.

The word *Gordian*
enters the debate,
the noun *knot*,

we glimpse Alex –
ander, his resolute
unhesitating sword,
example, surely,

to us all, all
those centuries
of example... You're
tempted? Some bait.

Take your hour.
Long until night.
The rabbit ever
motionless, born
playboy that rabbit.
Stone, lithe stone
invigorates reams
of the inanimate

as, wait, over
the left shoulder
comes another
solution to the Gordian
Knot conundrum:

soundless, never
looking back, I
bid goodbye to
my grassy plot
among the whins.

Today's lesson: Alex-
ander's sword was
right for him, *treise
leis*, but didn't,
not for a moment,
exhaust the lexicon,
superabundant,
of choice... Moment
of greatest release?

Rejecting temptation
to look back. Moment
of keenest frisson?
Lowering the gun.

What are you on about?
What, tell us, *what are you like*?
The morning walk, the hunt.
The bliss. Bliss of unknowing.

26 | Embrace

Sunday, Sunday after the burial,
I sit in his fireside chair, a choice,
and waited. Didn't know I was
waiting – but did – plummet level.

Won't take long: feral undertow,
then his grip – forged – about my chest
and shoulders, ramsacks my innards:
I sit there sapless, a nothing, couldn't
push a cat off a stool – ghosts
need time to learn their *élan nouveaux*?

So set your glass of wine on the floor,
mime composure – the widow present,
the child, two or three, say, more.
'Are you all right there?' 'In my tent'.

Piecemeal, I return to myself, part
of myself, the ordained ghost grip,
takes something away, no mistake about that,
from this out I'd boast an interior gimp.

What was he conveying to you in
that swoop, unimaginable coupling?
Was he saying, simply – 'The pain, pain
of it all – gone now – thanks for the minding'?

Was he saying – 'Here pure song-
fest – no less – dancing all night long'?

Or just bidding – rough neophyte ghost –
hello and goodbye, wanderer's heist?

Forty years since. The track on me
yet. Don't- ever-fade-embrace. Happily.

27 | Initiant

So what's with the snake then, tell us?
A rude slap early across the puss
left the poor lad in a horrid nonplus!

Tail-dance followed, lifting from the forest
pool in colours of the morning,
reaming you qua Imperial Edict
but you're still loth to bow, cadging
a lift to compliant muff, spent
before arrival, let's not discuss it.

Flirting of an afternoon, shyly –
She, yes, does *shyly*, some repertoire,
surfacing, Mistress of Your River,
April-fleck'd, hey, China, let's play –

She's The Belly Dancer of Forgiveness.

Next, snake inside you, found a womb
and nearing full-term, shown her
on the scan, She's single-limb
flourish, stashed in velouté interior
dusk, no hurry on her, contain-
ment the key, snake always knows when.

That'll be the day. Uproar galore.
Ticker-tape? Time's Square? Piccadilly?
No, no. Nor The Fair of Ringaskiddy.
For Swaddling Clothes our Forest Floor,
for Marriage Feast the Holy Door.

28 | Poppy's Leavetaking

Imbued, wise beyond
Delphi, she's throwaway,
every operatic red
waxing tufa grey,

unbridles all her
suspenders, most intimate
furbelows, flings herself at
the clay, the paramour
and sumptuary clay,

never more beautiful,
seem'd to this observer,
triumphant funereal
she bade me give ear –

'Here be Leavetaking,
take heed, it's for free,
dough for the baking,
gum from the tree,

only one way to go –
toss all to the wind,
nuthin' left, nuthin' left –
you're echoes – of tomorrow –
hummin' under your breath,
sh'd it please, M'Lud,
of the sun on the snow.'

Of a sudden her drift
was a working pulse.

'Nuthin' left, nuthin' left,
how you know, Poppy,
nuthin' left, nuthin' else?'

'Moment tells,' said Poppy,
that voice a windburned lyre,
'Moment will always tell.
That's a truth. And a fire.'
I shut up for a while.

We hung there,
could be quiet forever,
that colour suss,
shored endeavour.

'Any other news?'
Was it doughty silence
left you afeared?

'Only the one,'
came Poppy, from her Cleopatrine
daisybells carnage of reds
oiling, ogling, the paramour clay,
'only the one, an' ever the one,
an' them cuttin' the corn in Creeshlough the day.'

29 | Found In A Suitcase

While you were away we met,
as often before. I suppose love.
You've on your best suit,
a white dog helps us
build in the mouth of the wave.

I was told once you must
build there the fortress with moat
and drawbridge, sentries,
a weather of still alert: else
nothing to keep back the wave.

30 | Observations

Tabled by a window,
toy-snake says – 'Hello.'

Hen-harrier, ranging freely,
targets the ould enemy,

patient by dusk, dives
for the kill, cracks
her neck against the glass.

Aroused, you discover
the lovely bird, caress
in dismay, inter,
tint of hugger-mugger,
langled obsequies.

        *****

Next morning, shaken
eye. The dead bird
sleeps. Pet talisman,
snake enjoys the sideboard.

Open the hall-door,
step into the light,
bathe in the summer,
meet the bird's mate,
house-height hover,
on orange alert.

Everything in check.
Sorry for your trouble,

not at my beck.
A rudder-tail
caresses your shy neck.

Indicted bows; Bereaved – fine
sombre arc, departs the scene.

31 | At Butt of the Lane

I remarked the hawk, high in the sky,
slowed my step – how raptor excites,
came to a stop, hawk now on the way,
well on the way, to eagle size:

so – fly-past – for you? Whiff
of fear took me, left, I held where
I'd landed, shedding roods of safe
ground, at speed no solitary tether

left of shopping-lists, diesel, tax,
such-like, the bird's now one-wing
bird, power-wing; says bird – 'Relax,
just pay attention, okay, everything

in this display's for you to win, lose,
cherish, spend, *petit repas*, come
tomorrow look for wilder menus,
we test appetites, Mystery's the name.'

The one wing – look – now transparent.
'Enjoy this window,' said bird, 'on every
azure ever stirred. While you're at it,
sample memories of the yet to be.'

The bird's gone, they don't overwrite,
these raptors at butt of the lane,
show you the truth, ask you to note,
leave you to sip the wine.

32 | The Honey

You've heard the laughter of shadows.
And, well you know, the honey knows.

Spoonful of honey, spoon
swimming towards your lips
but always some lapse,
it refuses to happen.

A week ago the bowl
of blackberries, fattest
ever, chosen, the pile
so steep a dozen tumble,
skitter out of sight.

And – hard to forget –
how often, the bed made,
the beautiful woman's protest,
disturbed eyes open wide,
'Why is it you always –
are you afraid of summer? –

why is it you always
send me away? Winter
more your time of year?'

Late in the day now.
Listen: the laughter of shadows.
Attend: the honey flow...

33 | *Brosna* means 'kindling', red *brosna* 'a kind of verse'

Even as once in love I fell,
I became a prize *brosna* junkie,
still don't know why, well
maybe I do, we know not what we...

No ditch was safe – blackthorn,
hazel, furze, dessicated briar,
I brought that woman home the wood –
what with clay, weed, scutch-grass forlorn,
fox-glove remnants, there was madness –
quelle gaucherie, o, ma Cherie –
but I couldn't, no, couldn't be stopped,
that's Love, ain't it, the poor blood on fire.

She watched, idle, amazed, took
it all as her due – and, innocent
affliction, knew it would pass, it
did, just a window. So. A look.

But its beating heart? To this day
(the scullery bravely served as Kind-
ling Depot) I remember an odour
pervading the house, frankly regal
breath of the soil, humus and wand:
therein singing , cooly, cooly fateful,
the sinuous sweetness of decay.

34 | Immersion

That blood be mine?
Modest, shameless,
the forefinger's
triple-incision
lisps come-on –
Sip, Warrior,
your vino veritas.

Later, pike-soup,
sit myself down
to eat it
and drink it;

uttering *Grace*
I smell of the lake,
tremble a bit.

35 | Those Ants

You weren't aware of the ants –
those pellets of instinct – nesting
in the spine of your Book of Days

until you saw them, processional,
get out o' there, and fast, their patience
at an end, you won't forget that,

the impetus, quiet, patina of affront,
a howl lifted in you to watch
them go, and a gush of knowledge:

you met their decorum of giving
('Always yield to the one with the load'),
ceremonious burial of kindred,
salutary counsel for grasshoppers,

hammer after the hatchet knew
their niceties of communication to be
an art form, you knew it all,

knew you'd thrown gold away,
knew gold is the price you pay.

36 | The Possible

'Oh, they let me out
a few times, y'know.'
'After *Tug*?' Me woman
way ahead on points.
'After *Tug*', I allow:
merry as a cricket,
snatch a riposte –
'But no tellin', none
what might happen!'

That does it all right.
Bindertwine blues.
Bites. The love-bite.
Barcarole dews...

No tellin', Bella,
what might happen –

37 | La Vie Bohème

In every mortal male a peeler hives.
I'd spurned a wealth of marchés
where that peeler-male held rule,
sniffed his baton, heard a cell-door
click. Now – *mulier cantat* – I'd
found my saviour. Comely late-thirties,
eyes of borage blue, everything about
her said – 'I know your need
before you loose a word.' D'accord!

It was, believe me you, the best
of times, my felon basket, my eggs,
my butter, my milk, my Chevre,
my Gouda and my Camembert...

Such seasons, all know, must
last forever, their sunlit largesse,
but came a day, a reckoning,
a beckoning, a look, woman's
look, hard to beat, woman's look.

I had perfected a saunter, my
deportment an immaculate
conception. And I'm savouring
what cheese today, mon ami,
morceau, peut-être, of Brie, when –
watch it – Madame's eyes are on
alert, from her Supervisor's raised
desk engage me. I took the hit,
slowed, *rapidment*, to a halt.
And now a stasis moment: bathe,

Traveller in it; her eyes, those eyes,
replete, such braided knowing
I may never again meet this side
eternity, such sotto voce

reprimand: all that, confidante,
takes micro-seconds. Whirl next
in which, I swear, we're plighted lovers,
an ample and delicious nest of spiceries
ours to share all summer long –
but let's not ask too much of Fortune.

Did I nod or did I bow or –
nothing formal, acquiescence,
that tilt of nod, yes, but surely
more, more, much, much more,
the note must be salute, blessing,
infinities of deference, clarion
statement of the one gospel by
which I've, stumbling, ever sought
to live and die: somehow or other,
it is not in women, *dulces
et amabiles*, not in woman
the peeler for to be...

Mulier, says Good Master Will,
from the Latin *mollis*, meaning *tender*,
wonder if you ever made it to
rue Biscornet, Maestro, love, love
to have heard your discourse on
my saviour of the Bonne Marché.

38 | Uncle Tim
In memory of TG

A strapping lad of twenty
and a bare-legged child
step it up Ardlow Hill –

'Do you not remember, man?
A winter day, the whole
country covered with snow' –

I remember now you're gone:
the quiet underfoot, talk
scarce but breath conversable,
from Bessie's Tom's wood-smoke,
Bradley's goats, the odd crow,
we're bound for the brow,
there's no looking back.

On the brow we pause,
your big hand firming mine,
turn to meet the view.
Gently it comes, takes us,
the bosomed white, all sides,
all sides the bosomed white.

39 | Such A Time With The Swan

No talisman, China, none,
no prayer, to stay the visit:
plumage black when first we meet,
She rides, triumphal, a compliant Acheron,
the serial silence, four-poster, post-
post-modern, for you, you alone.

Next trip, She's open wound –
don't run, there's no cover:
from idle blue the harrier plummet,
document in gob, brake to hover,
hurl the writ, javelin caveat,
Jug-jug, it sings, jugular bound.
(Would you have read it?)

So, so richly laden Her hoard.
The Intended, young, tutored
was by a spray of down. Infant feather,
pianissimo, would induce aid,
massage every last fold of weather,
body and soul, transform Bride
to the pitch she must depart. Did.
In a wisp of Swan the gentlest sword.

Silence now the rack. And the road.
Reynard shows, hooped black-and-green,
trailed by a flock of reed bunting
(bantam size for the hard of seeing),
cherish, while breath holds, that fox's keen.

They lead me to Her shore cave.
Comfortable in white, and grown

prodigiously, She broods. The heap
of driftwood is nest, sculpted wave,
the silence here, listen, Quiet's own.
She nods me close. And I obey,
surrender to that breast's fierce dawn.
Swan's neck descends, unconscionably
mild, enfolds me, and I sleep.

40 | Her Bright Scissors
(verses on reaching four score)

They float, weightless, look,
Flaneur, salute, revere this blaze
like no other, learn to walk,
shift the slouch from your days.

Only the one grand cru,
scour the vineyards
from here to Peru.

How they glow.
Obeisance,
Lady Atropos.

À bientôt. À bientôt.

41 | The Storm

A skelp of leafy ash
slips her mooring,

becomes one
with the storm, the un-
appeasable,

in whose arms you've
passed many a season,

Sense and Reason
hostages to Fortune.

42 | The Portrait Hour

He finds me using
a stick (ash), a band
of light green netting
around the hand
which holds the stick.

I say – 'I'm a mite.
Carrying a story. And
one of the stories is Death.'

Am I laying it on?
He says little. Nothing.
He's all eye. Crayon.

Forgotten when,
I begin to babble –
the women, the children.
Soon go still.